Welcome, fellow entrepreneur! Your journey starts now. This ebook equips you with the critical things you need keep in mind to successfully navigate the exciting and challenging world of entrepreneurship.

Mansi Gupta,
Business Coach

About me

Hi, I am Mansi Gupta.
I'm a business coach and transformation expert with over 18 years under my belt. I've seen it all, from finance and consulting to transformations and training. Not only that, I've also started three successful businesses of my own!

Here's a sneak peek into my world:
- Trained over 100 large companies on how to grow their businesses through my corporate training company.
- Ran a large-scale distribution network across North India for several well-known brands through my retail distributor venture.
- Redefined early education through a children's education startup that I successfully exited, leaving behind a memorable legacy.
- Guided and empowered solopreneurs, medium enterprises, and even big corporations to reach their full potential.
- Shared my knowledge as a visiting faculty member at prestigious MBA institutes like IIM-Lucknow and TAPMI.
- Developed a deep expertise in systems, HR, and finance analytics during my time at HDFC Bank and as a Director at Nagarro.

What fuels my fire? You guessed it – processes and outcomes! I'm passionate about helping businesses achieve their goals through efficient systems and measurable results.
So, if you're looking to transform your business, get in touch with me. Let's chat and see how I can help you reach your full potential!

Business Coaching | www.mansigupta.in

How to use this book

No Shortcuts, Just Action: Your Roadmap to Building a Thriving Business in India

Forget fancy formulas and instant success promises. This book is your practical guide to building a thriving business in India, one step at a time. No magic tricks, just clear steps and actionable tips to help you navigate the journey.

Think of this as your personal checklist, not a pre-written script. Each chapter tackles a crucial aspect of starting and growing your business, from defining your vision to managing your time like a pro. But the real magic happens when you take these tips and make them your own.

This book simplifies the big picture, but the journey is yours to explore. We show you the path, but you choose the pace and the tools. Each tip is a stepping stone, not a shortcut. The "how" and "why" behind each step - that's where your personal learning begins.

Ready to unleash your entrepreneurial spirit? Here's how this book can guide your journey:

- Chart Your Course: Each chapter acts as a compass, helping you define your vision, values, and goals. It's your starting point, not a pre-determined path.
- Embrace Experimentation: Every tip is a suggestion, an invitation to explore and adapt it to your unique business. There's no one-size-fits-all approach, so make it your own.
- Fuel Your Learning: We point you towards valuable resources like online courses, tools, and even potential mentors. But the real learning happens when you delve deeper, seek out knowledge, and connect with like-minded individuals.
- Celebrate Your Progress: This book is your companion, not a drill sergeant. Track your milestones, celebrate your achievements, and learn from setbacks. It's a journey of self-discovery, not a race to the finish line.

...contd.

...contd.

Remember, this book is a springboard, not a magic carpet. The power to build your dream business lies within you. Use this guide to find your direction, fuel your learning, and embrace the adventure of entrepreneurship.

Want to save time and get expert guidance? Consider partnering with a business coach. Think of them as your seasoned companion on this journey, someone who can:

- Simplify complex concepts and tailor them to your specific needs. No one-size-fits-all approaches here!
- Offer valuable insights and keep you motivated. Stay focused and avoid getting lost in the details.
- Celebrate your wins and hold you accountable. Every step counts, and your coach will be there to support you.

Remember, this book is your starting point, not the finish line. The real success lies in your action, your learning, and your unwavering commitment to your vision. So, grab your pen, open your mind, and get ready to build your dream business.

No shortcuts, just Crystal Clarity and your own unique path to success. Go forth and make it remarkable!

PART 1:

Building Your Foundation

1.

Craft a Crystal-Clear Vision

- **Envision the Future:** What do you want your business to achieve in the vibrant Indian market? Who do you want to serve and how will you improve their lives?

- **Define Your Values:** What principles are fundamental to your business? Integrity, innovation, customer focus - choose values that guide your decision-making and actions.

- **Set SMART Goals:** Break down your vision into achievable milestones. Set SMART goals (Specific, Measurable, Achievable, Relevant, and Time-bound) to stay on track and track your progress.

2.

Embrace Resilience and Adaptability

- **Challenges are Inevitable**: Embrace setbacks as opportunities to learn and grow. Analyze what went wrong, adapt your strategy, and keep moving forward.

- **Be Flexible**: The Indian market is dynamic. Stay informed about industry trends, adapt your offerings as needed, and be prepared to pivot when necessary.

- **Develop Resilience**: Cultivate a growth mindset. Believe in your ability to overcome obstacles and learn from mistakes.

3.

Master Time Management

- **Prioritize ruthlessly:** Identify the tasks that move your business forward and focus your energy on them.

- **Delegate effectively:** Don't try to do everything yourself. Empower your team members and delegate tasks to free up your time for strategic thinking.

- **Maintain a healthy balance:** Allocate time for work, rest, and personal pursuits. A balanced schedule leads to long-term success and well-being.

PART 2:

Building Your Team and Strategy

4.

Build a Strong and Dynamic Team

- **Hire for Talent and Value Alignment:** Look for individuals with the skills and experience your business needs, but also ensure they share your values and vision.

- **Foster Collaboration:** Encourage open communication, teamwork, and a supportive environment where everyone feels valued and respected.

- **Invest in Development:** Provide opportunities for your team to learn and grow through training, workshops, and mentoring programs.

5.

Develop a Robust Business Plan

- **Chart Your Course:** Define your target market, competitive landscape, marketing strategy, financial projections, and operational plan.

- **Seek Feedback:** Share your plan with trusted advisors and mentors for constructive criticism and valuable insights.

- **Continually Adapt:** Your plan is a living document. Update it regularly to reflect changes in your business or the market.

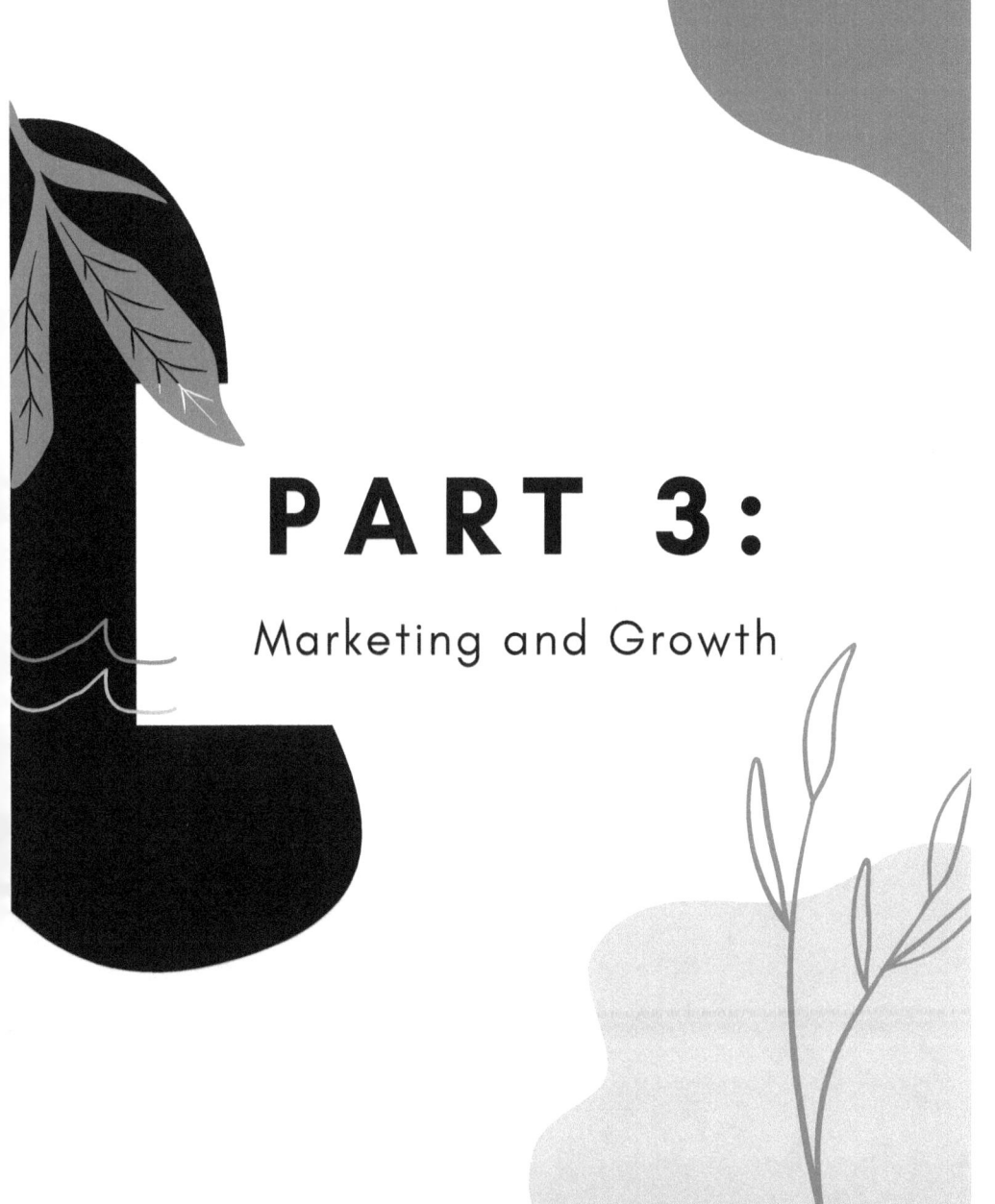

PART 3:

Marketing and Growth

6.

Understand Your Market and Customer Base

- **Know Your Audience:** Conduct thorough research to understand your ideal customers, their needs, wants, and pain points.

- **Build Relationships:** Engage with your customers, listen to their feedback, and understand their buying journey.

- **Gather Data:** Utilize tools like Google Trends and Facebook Insights to gather valuable data and inform your marketing strategies.

7.

Create a Compelling Brand Identity

- **Craft a Consistent Image:** Develop a brand identity that reflects your values and resonates with your target audience.

- **Tell Your Story:** Use your brand story to connect with your customers on an emotional level and build a loyal following.

- **Maintain Consistency:** Ensure your brand identity is consistent across all platforms, from your website to your social media profiles.

8.

Leverage the Power of Digital Marketing

- **Reach Your Audience Online:** Utilize social media platforms like Facebook and Instagram to connect with your target audience and promote your brand.

- **Embrace Content Marketing:** Create valuable content that educates, informs, and engages your audience. There are many online tools that can be used to manage your campaigns effectively.

- **Track and Analyze:** Monitor your marketing performance and use data to optimize your campaigns and maximize ROI.

PART 4:

Continuous Learning and Growth

9.

Embrace Innovation and Technology

- **Stay Ahead of the Curve:** Keep yourself informed about emerging technologies relevant to your industry and explore ways to integrate them into your business.

- **Automate Tasks:** Utilize technology to automate repetitive tasks, freeing up your time to focus on strategic initiatives.

- **Invest in Customer Experience:** Implement tools that help you improve customer service and build stronger relationships.

10.

Invest in Continuous Learning and Personal Growth

- **Challenge Yourself:** Step outside your comfort zone and embrace new challenges to expand your knowledge and skillset.

- **Seek Mentorship:** Connect with experienced entrepreneurs and learn from their wisdom and insights.

- **Practice Self-Care:** Prioritize your mental and physical well-being. There are many online tools that can help you manage stress and maintain focus.

In conclusion, your entrepreneurial journey is a path of limitless possibilities. Armed with the strategies and resources laid out in this book, coupled with your unwavering dedication and passion, you have the power to turn your vision into a thriving reality.

Remember, success is a continuous journey, not a destination. Embrace the challenges, celebrate the victories, and never stop learning and growing.

With Crystal Clarity guiding your way, you can achieve remarkable success and make a positive impact on the Indian market.

Now, go forth and unleash your entrepreneurial spirit!

Mansi Gupta,
Business Coach

Free Resources for Budding Businesses: Your Entrepreneurial Toolkit

Fuel your startup with this curated list of free resources, designed to empower your journey from idea to empire.

Online Courses:
- Khan Academy: Master the fundamentals of business and entrepreneurship with free courses on everything from finance and marketing to accounting and management.
- Startup School: Dive deep into the world of startups with this platform offering free courses and resources tailored specifically for aspiring entrepreneurs.
- OpenSesame: Explore a vast library of free and paid online courses covering business essentials, marketing strategies, and leadership skills.
- edX: Partner with top universities and institutions like MIT and Harvard to access free and affordable courses on various business topics.
- Coursera: Learn from industry experts and renowned professors in free online courses spanning marketing, finance, technology, and more.

Productivity and Management Tools:
- Trello: Organize your team, manage projects, and collaborate seamlessly with this free project management tool.
- Asana: Track tasks, set deadlines, and monitor progress with this user-friendly platform, boosting your team's efficiency.
- Zoho Projects: Manage projects, collaborate with clients, and track progress with this free project management solution for small teams.
- Google Workspace: Access essential tools like Gmail, Docs, Sheets, and Calendar for free, streamlining communication and collaboration within your business.
- Slack: Connect with your team, share files, and collaborate in real-time with this free communication platform.

Marketing and Branding:
- Canva: Design stunning visuals for your brand, including logos, social media graphics, and presentations, with this free and easy-to-use platform.
- Adobe Spark: Create professional-looking videos, social media posts, and landing pages with this free design tool from Adobe.
- Hootsuite: Schedule social media posts, track engagement, and manage multiple accounts from one place with this free platform.
- Google Analytics: Gain valuable insights into your website traffic, audience demographics, and user behavior to optimize your marketing strategies.
- Mailchimp: Build and manage your email list, send newsletters, and track campaign performance with this free email marketing tool.

Financial Management and Legal Resources:
- Mint: Track your income and expenses, set budgets, and gain financial insights with this free budgeting and finance management app.
- Wave Accounting: Manage your finances, send invoices, track expenses, and generate reports with this free accounting software for small businesses.
- SCORE: Connect with experienced mentors and access free resources on business planning, marketing, and financial management.
- Startup Genome: Gain access to valuable data and research on startup ecosystems, funding trends, and industry insights.

Reading Resources for New Entrepreneurs:
- The Lean Startup: Eric Ries's guide to building startups with minimal resources and validated learning.
- Zero to One: Peter Thiel's exploration of creating monopolies and disrupting established industries.
- The Hard Thing About Hard Things: Ben Horowitz's honest and insightful look at the challenges and rewards of building a company.
- Traction: Gabriel Weinberg and Justin Mares's practical guide to identifying and validating your startup's growth channel.
- Hooked: Nir Eyal's analysis of what makes products addictive and how to apply those principles to your business.

Remember, this is just the tip of the iceberg! As you explore your entrepreneurial journey, keep learning, adapting, and connecting with other aspiring founders. These resources are your launchpad, your fuel, and your companions on the path to success.

NOTES

NOTES

THINGS TO DO

THINGS TO DO